The All About Series
All About ... Canadian Animals

Raccoons

Barb McDermott and Gail McKeown
Reidmore Books

Reidmore Books Inc.

For more information contact
Nelson Thomson Learning,
1120 Birchmount Road,
Scarborough, Ontario,
M1K 5G4.
Or you can visit our
internet site at
http://www.nelson.com

Printed and bound in Canada
3 4 5 03 02 01

Canadian Cataloguing in Publication Data
McDermott, Barb.
All about Canadian animals : raccoons

(All about series)
Includes index.
ISBN 1-896132-05-7

1. Raccoons--Canada--Juvenile literature. I. McKeown, Gail. II. Title. III. Series: McDermott, Barb. All about series.
QL737.C26M32 1998   j599.76'32'0971   C98-910180-0

About the Authors

Barb McDermott and Gail McKeown are highly experienced kindergarten teachers living in Ontario. Both hold Bachelor of Arts and Bachelor of Education degrees, Early Childhood diplomas, specialist certificates in Primary Education, and have completed qualification courses in Special Education. As well, Gail has a specialist certificate in Reading and Visual Arts, and Barb has one in Guidance.

Credits

Editorial: Leah-Ann Lymer, Scott Woodley
Illustration, design and layout: Bruno Enderlin, David Strand

Photo Credits

Entries are by page number, coded as follows:
T=Top, B=Bottom, L=Left, R=Right
Abbreviations: VU=Visuals Unlimited
Cover and stamp photo
VU/Tom J. Ulrich
Page
1 VU/Ken Lucas
3 VU/Barbara Gerlach
5 VU/R. Lindholm
7 VU/Ron Spomer
9 VU/Joe McDonald
11 VU/Stephen Lang
13 Omni Photo/Image Network Inc.
15 VU/Joe McDonald
17 VU/Maslowski
19 VU/Joe McDonald
21 VU/R. Knolan Benfield, Jr.
23 VU/Joe McDonald
25 VU/R. Al Simpson
27 VU/Buff and Gerald Corsi

We have made every effort to identify and credit the sources of all photographs, illustrations, and information used in this book. Reidmore Books appreciates any further information or corrections; acknowledgment will be given in subsequent editions.

Table of Contents

(All about what's in the book)

Appearance	page 1
Habitat	page 4
Diet	page 8
Predators	page 12
Offspring	page 14
Adaptation	page 18
Special Characteristics	page 22
Summary	page 26
Glossary	page 28
Index	page 29

Appearance
(All about what raccoons look like)

Raccoons are **mammals** of the **freshwater** lakes.

Raccoons can live 10 years.

Raccoons have a band of black fur on their face.

Raccoons look like they are wearing a black **mask**.

Raccoons have a pointy face and a big head.

CANADA

Canada

A Raccoon

Appearance
(All about what raccoons look like)

Raccoons can be 85 cm long.

Raccoons have 2 fur coats.

Raccoons have a thick, brown undercoat.

Raccoons have a long, brown, grey, and black outer coat.

Raccoons have a long, bushy, ringed tail.

Raccoons have 5 to 10 black rings on their tail.

Raccoons can weigh 5 to 12 kg.

Canada

Raccoons Have a Mask and a Ringed Tail

3

Habitat
(All about where raccoons live)

Raccoons live in forests.

Raccoons live near water.

Raccoons live on the ground and in trees.

Raccoons sleep in a **den** during the day.

The den is made from a hollow log, a tree stump, or an old muskrat den.

Raccoons also live in cities close to people.

Raccoon Babies at Their Den

Raccoons

Habitat
(All about where raccoons live)

Raccoon **territory** is about 4 to 100 hectares.

Raccoons are active most of the year.

Raccoons sleep for part of the winter in their dens.

Raccoons live alone.

A Raccoon in a Tree

Diet
(All about what raccoons eat)

Raccoons are **omnivores**.

Raccoons will eat just about anything!

Raccoons like to play with their food before eating it.

Raccoons hunt for food at night.

Raccoons can travel 16 km looking for food.

A Raccoon Eating a Fish

Diet
(All about what raccoons eat)

Raccoons eat fish, crayfish, frogs, turtles, garter snakes, and snails.

Raccoons also eat berries, nuts, seeds, insects, corn, fruit, mice, and bird's eggs.

Raccoons have sharp teeth for biting.

Canada

A Raccoon Eating an Apple

Predators

(All about the enemies of raccoons)

The enemies of raccoons are wolves, red foxes, lynxes, coyotes, and dogs.

The enemy of raccoon babies is the great horned owl.

Raccoons climb trees to **escape** from their enemies.

People can be enemies to raccoons, too.

A Great Horned Owl

Offspring
(All about raccoon babies)

Raccoon babies are called kittens.

Kittens cannot see or hear when they are born.

Kittens do not have a masked face or ringed tail when they are born.

A Raccoon Kitten

Offspring
(All about raccoon babies)

Raccoons have 3 to 4 babies in the spring.

Raccoons have 1 **litter** every year.

Kittens drink milk from their mother.

Kittens open their eyes when they are 20 days old.

Kittens stay in their den for 8 to 10 weeks.

A Mother and Her Kittens

Adaptation
(All about how raccoons live in their world)

Raccoons use their tail to help them balance.

Raccoons wrap their tail around themselves like a blanket when they sleep.

Raccoons can climb down a tree head first.

Raccoons are good climbers and swimmers.

The Tail Gives Balance

Adaptation
(All about how raccoons live in their world)

Raccoons are **nocturnal** animals.

Raccoons can see well at night.

Raccoon eyes can shine at night.

Raccoon Eyes Can Shine

21

Special Characteristics
(All about what makes raccoons interesting)

Raccoons are **curious** and clever.

Raccoons use their sharp claws to help themselves to climb.

Raccoons can open just about anything with their **paws**.

Raccoons learn a lot about their world by exploring.

Canada

A Raccoon Opening a Shell with Its Paws

Special Characteristics
(All about what makes raccoons interesting)

Raccoons have a good sense of smell, touch, and hearing.

Raccoons sometimes go into garbage cans to look for food.

Raccoons snarl, whistle, growl, and chatter with their teeth.

A Raccoon Looking for Food

Summary
(All about the ending)

Raccoons have a long, bushy, ringed tail and a black mask.

Raccoons are clever animals who can live in many different places.

Raccoons are truly amazing animals ... that live in Canada!

Raccoons Are Clever

Glossary
(All about what the words mean)

curious (page 22)
Curious means eager to learn about things.

den (page 4)
A den is a place where a wild animal lives.

escape (page 12)
To escape is to get away.

freshwater (page 1)
Freshwater is water with no salt.

litter (page 16)
A litter is babies born at the same time from the same mother.

mammals (page 1)
Mammals are animals who feed their babies milk.

mask (page 1)
A mask is a covering that hides the face.

nocturnal (page 20)
Nocturnal means active during the night instead of during the day.

omnivores (page 8)
Omnivores are animals who eat plants and meat.

paws (page 22)
Paws are the feet of 4-footed animals with claws.

territory (page 6)
A territory is an area of land.